CREATING YOUR OWN ECONOMY
STUDY GUIDE

Copyright © 2025 by Dr. Dave Martin

Published by AVAIL

All rights reserved. No portion of this book may be reproduced, stored in a retrieval system, or transmitted in any form or by any means—electronic, mechanical, photocopy, recording, scanning, or other—except for brief quotations in critical reviews or articles, without prior written permission of the author.

Scripture quotations marked KJV are taken from the King James Version of the Bible. Public domain. | Scripture quotations marked NIV are taken from the Holy Bible, New International Version®, NIV®. Copyright © 1973, 1978, 1984, 2011 by Biblica, Inc.™ Used by permission of Zondervan. All rights reserved worldwide. www.zondervan.com. The "NIV" and "New International Version" are trademarks registered in the United States Patent and Trademark Office by Biblica, Inc.™ | Scripture quotations marked MSG are taken from THE MESSAGE, copyright © 1993, 1994, 1995, 1996, 2000, 2001, 2002 by Eugene H. Peterson. Used by permission of NavPress. All rights reserved. Represented by Tyndale House Publishers, Inc. | Scripture quotations marked ESV are from the ESV® Bible (The Holy Bible, English Standard Version®). ESV® Text Edition: 2016. Copyright © 2001 by Crossway, a publishing ministry of Good News Publishers. The ESV® text has been reproduced in cooperation with and by permission of Good News Publishers. Unauthorized reproduction of this publication is prohibited. All rights reserved.

For foreign and subsidiary rights, contact the author.

Cover design by: Sara Young
Cover photo by: Kyla Stewart

ISBN: 978-1-964794-43-3   1 2 3 4 5 6 7 8 9 10

Printed in the United States of America.

DR. DAVE MARTIN

CREATING YOUR OWN ECONOMY

A GUIDE TO FINANCIAL FREEDOM AND GENEROUS LIVING

STUDY GUIDE

AVAIL

CONTENTS

CHAPTER 1. **Extinguish Your Limiting Beliefs** 6

CHAPTER 2. **Understand God's Nature** 12

CHAPTER 3. **Create the Right Mindset** 18

CHAPTER 4. **Examine Your Heart** 24

CHAPTER 5. **Set Your Priorities** 30

CHAPTER 6. **Pay Your Tithe** 36

CHAPTER 7. **Determine to Do the Work** 42

CHAPTER 8. **Give and Prosper** 48

CHAPTER 9. **Establish Your True Motives** 54

CHAPTER 1

EXTINGUISH YOUR LIMITING BELIEFS

> THE LORD WANTS THE BEST FOR HIS CHILDREN, BUT HIS BEST ALWAYS INVOLVES MORE THAN JUST MATERIAL SATISFACTION.

REVIEW, REFLECT, AND RESPOND

As you read Chapter 1: "Extinguish Your Limiting Beliefs" in *Creating Your Own Economy*, review, reflect on, and respond to the text by answering the following questions.

How do your biblical beliefs about money shape your mindset? What limiting beliefs about finances have you identified, and how have they influenced your actions and decisions?

_____
_____
_____
_____
_____

Before reading this book, how much did you know about God's financial principles and the guidance He provides in His Word?

_____
_____
_____
_____
_____

How have your own financial struggles contributed to your beliefs about money or challenged your faith in what the Word of God says about it?

_____
_____
_____
_____
_____

> *"For the love of money is a root of all kinds of evil. Some people, eager for money, have wandered from the faith and pierced themselves with many griefs."*
>
> —**1 Timothy 6:10 (NIV)**

Consider the scripture above and answer the following questions:

Why do you think many Christians equate money with sinfulness, and how might this misunderstanding hinder their ability to use resources for God's purposes?

_____

_____

_____

_____

_____

_____

_____

Reflect on your own beliefs about money. Have you ever avoided pursuing financial success out of fear that it might compromise your faith? Where did that fear come from?

_____

_____

_____

_____

_____

_____

_____

How has the culture around you shaped your views on money and prosperity?

_____
_____
_____
_____
_____
_____

Have you ever known a believer who put money above God, and what kind of fruit did this produce?

_____
_____
_____
_____
_____
_____

Review the three primary limiting beliefs listed in this chapter (poverty is a form of godliness, material wealth defines your prosperity, and money is evil). Which resonates with you the most, and why?

_____
_____
_____
_____
_____
_____

What about poverty isn't godly? How might poverty actually work against the purposes of God in your life?

_____
_____
_____
_____
_____
_____
_____
_____
_____
_____

In what ways have you seen prosperity in your life outside of material wealth? What experiences do you have with "hoarding" versus using your resources to bless others?

_____
_____
_____
_____
_____
_____
_____
_____
_____
_____

In what ways have wrong teachings about money impacted the way you handle money and your financial situation?

_____
_____

What changes do you feel called to make in your mindset or habits after reading this chapter?

In your own words, what's the difference between a kingdom economy and a worldly economy?

CHAPTER 2

UNDERSTAND GOD'S NATURE

> IF WEALTH IS SO WRONG FOR CHRISTIANS, WHY WOULD GOD GIVE HIS PEOPLE THE POWER TO CREATE IT?

REVIEW, REFLECT, AND RESPOND

As you read Chapter 2: "Understand God's Nature" in *Creating Your Own Economy,* review, reflect on, and respond to the text by answering the following questions.

Have you ever faced a time when financial challenges hindered your ability to give as God calls you to? How has that experience shaped your understanding of His character, and where do you stand with this now?

_____
_____
_____
_____
_____
_____
_____
_____

Consider all the ways God blessed Abraham described in this chapter. What did you learn from this, and how could you apply it to your own life?

_____
_____
_____
_____
_____
_____
_____
_____

What unique skills, talents, and abilities has God entrusted to you to bless and serve others? How have you seen Him use them in your life so far, and how might you seek His guidance to use them more intentionally today?

_____
_____
_____
_____
_____
_____
_____

> *"But remember the Lord your God, for it is he who gives you the ability to produce wealth, and so confirms his covenant, which he swore to your ancestors, as it is today."*
>
> **—Deuteronomy 8:18 (NIV)**

Consider the scripture above and answer the following questions:

If God's provision of wealth is tied to His covenant and purpose, how does this influence the way you view and use your financial resources?

_____
_____
_____
_____
_____
_____
_____

What role does pride play in neglecting God as the source of our wealth? How might underlying beliefs about self-reliance be tied to erroneous views about wealth as unbiblical or unholy?

_____
_____
_____
_____
_____

God is a God of abundance, not scarcity. Reflect on an area of your life where you have adopted a scarcity mindset. How does this chapter challenge that mindset, and what are some practical steps you could take to break free from it?

_____
_____
_____
_____
_____

Describe what it means for money to be a "tool." Do you know any believers who keep money in its proper place—using it only as a tool—and in what ways are they an example of God's desire to empower us to get wealth?

_____
_____
_____
_____
_____

Think about the statement, "God doesn't mind if I have money as long as my money doesn't have me." How does this convict you about areas in your life where possessions might hold too much control?

_____
_____
_____
_____
_____
_____
_____
_____

What internal barriers—fear, doubt, or guilt—stop you from fully embracing God's desire to bless you? How ready and willing are you to surrender these to Him?

_____
_____
_____
_____
_____
_____
_____
_____

Consider the metaphor of the papaya seeds. How does this challenge you to consider what God can do with little, and how does it inspire you to be a faithful steward with your money?

_____
_____

In what ways has a "too good to be true" philosophy hindered you from living in prosperity?

How might delay contribute to unbelief about God's desire to prosper you? What did this chapter teach you about how delays don't mean God doesn't want you to live in abundance?

CHAPTER 3

CREATE THE RIGHT MINDSET

> A PERSON NEEDS A NEW HEART BEFORE HE CAN HAVE A NEW MIND.

REVIEW, REFLECT, AND RESPOND

As you read Chapter 3: "Create the Right Mindset" in *Creating Your Own Economy*, review, reflect on, and respond to the text by answering the following questions.

When you think about the power of your thoughts, what negative patterns do you recognize in your daily life? How have they impacted your faith, beliefs, and decisions?

_____
_____
_____
_____
_____
_____
_____
_____

Describe a moment when your perspective shifted from doubt to faith. What triggered this change, and how did it impact your actions and outcomes? How could you apply this experience to your finances?

_____
_____
_____
_____
_____
_____
_____
_____

What voices are speaking into your life about God's view of money? Are they discouraging you from believing God desires your abundance, or are they encouraging you?

_____
_____
_____
_____
_____
_____
_____
_____

> *"Do not conform to the pattern of this world, but be transformed by the renewing of your mind. Then you will be able to test and approve what God's will is—his good, pleasing and perfect will."*
>
> **—Romans 12:2 (NIV)**

Consider the scripture above and answer the following questions:

Are you in the practice of renewing your mind? What might it look and sound like to renew your mind so that your thoughts about money align with God's Word?

_____
_____
_____
_____
_____
_____

Why does renewing your mind illuminate God's will for areas of your life that feel uncertain or areas where you are stuck?

_____
_____
_____
_____
_____
_____

Why do you think a person's heart can change so quickly when it takes a lifetime to change a person's thinking? Why does the heart need to change before the mind can change?

_____
_____
_____
_____
_____
_____

When you consider God's promises, do you find yourself doubting their relevance to your life? Why or why not?

_____
_____
_____
_____
_____
_____

How can your current financial situation be traced back to your heart and your thinking?

_____
_____
_____
_____
_____
_____

How do you respond when your circumstances appear to contradict what you believe about God's desire for you to thrive? What does this reveal about your mindset?

_____
_____
_____
_____
_____
_____

How have doubt, guilt, or feelings of unworthiness affected your ability to receive God's blessings? What areas in your heart or mindset need healing to embrace His abundance fully?

_____
_____
_____
_____
_____
_____

How do you reconcile inevitable seasons of lack with God's will to prosper you?

_____
_____
_____
_____
_____
_____

Why do you think financial thinking is such a "sticky" issue for Christians, and why is it an issue that is particularly difficult to hand over to the Lord?

_____
_____
_____
_____
_____
_____
_____

In what ways might you be harboring earthly thinking about money disguised as kingdom thinking?

_____
_____
_____
_____
_____
_____
_____

CHAPTER 4

EXAMINE YOUR HEART

> THE TONGUE IS DESIGNED TO "REGURGITATE" THE CONTENT OF THE HEART.

REVIEW, REFLECT, AND RESPOND

As you read Chapter 4: "Examine Your Heart" in *Creating Your Own Economy*, review, reflect on, and respond to the text by answering the following questions.

What is the difference between the mind and the heart as it relates to the walk of a believer? Why is the heart more important for discovering hidden beliefs and attitudes about money?

_____
_____
_____
_____
_____
_____
_____

To what extent are you just listening to God's Word, and to what extent are you feasting on God's Word? In what ways does the condition of your heart reflect how you engage with and approach studying God's Word?

_____
_____
_____
_____
_____
_____
_____
_____

How would you evaluate yourself in fulfilling the prerequisite for seeing God's promise of prosperity come alive in your life—having His Word deeply rooted in your heart?

_____
_____
_____
_____
_____
_____

> ***"A good man brings good things out of the good stored up in him, and an evil man brings evil things out of the evil stored up in him."***
>
> **—Matthew 12:35 (NIV)**

Consider the scripture above and answer the following questions:

How do the words you speak in moments of financial frustration or pressure reflect what is stored in your heart?

_____
_____
_____
_____
_____
_____
_____
_____
_____

What are you storing up in your heart? Have you thoroughly searched your heart or asked God to search it for you?

_____
_____
_____
_____
_____

Consider the confessions in this chapter that reflect God's Word about finances. Which one resonates with you the most, and why does it speak to you personally? What steps do you need to take to consistently incorporate these confessions into your daily routine?

_____
_____
_____
_____
_____

What is your tongue exposing about what you truly believe about God and His ability to guide your life? Is there a phrase or confession you catch yourself repeating that doesn't reflect the true will of God?

_____
_____
_____
_____
_____

What confessions from God's Word do you make but don't actually believe? Why?

___

Faith often follows confessions from the Word of God. Which of your current confessions about money needs the most change, and what new confession grounded in God's truth can you start speaking to replace it?

___

How do you understand the process of "reprogramming" the hard drive of your mind? What do you expect that process to look like, and what expectations need adjusting before you can begin to see real results?

___

What might happen if you started reciting scripture out loud on a regular basis despite having no reason to expect a favorable outcome?

Explain why the power behind biblical confession isn't found in your words but rather in the words you speak from the mouth of God.

CHAPTER 5

SET YOUR PRIORITIES

> GOD NEVER BLESSES NOTHING. INSTEAD, HE ALWAYS BLESSES SOMETHING.

REVIEW, REFLECT, AND RESPOND

As you read Chapter 5: "Set Your Priorities" in *Creating Your Own Economy*, review, reflect on, and respond to the text by answering the following questions.

Reflect on the last week. Where did your time, energy, and focus go? What does this reveal about where God is in your priorities?

_____
_____
_____
_____
_____
_____
_____

Take a close look at all areas of your life—church, work, relationships, family, and finances. How do you demonstrate putting God first in each of these? Considering this, how confident do you believe the Lord is in entrusting His resources to you?

_____
_____
_____
_____
_____
_____
_____

What can you learn from Abraham and his decision to put God first in a radical act of obedience? Like Abraham, what action can you take to begin to activate God's promise of abundance?

_____
_____
_____
_____
_____
_____
_____
_____

> *"And God said, Let us make man in our image, after our likeness: and let them have dominion over the fish of the sea, and over the fowl of the air, and over the cattle, and over all the earth, and over every creeping thing that creepeth upon the earth."*
>
> **—Genesis 1:26 (KJV)**

Consider the scripture above and answer the following questions:

How does the truth that God has given humanity authority over creation challenge any limiting beliefs you might have about God's desire for you to receive and manage financial blessings?

_____
_____
_____
_____
_____

How far does your current stance on money deviate from the truth of this scripture? What is the link between our authority over the earth and God's intention to bless us?

How do our spiritual lives and material lives work together in harmony rather than conflict? Why should they be viewed as complementary rather than mutually exclusive?

Why might holding onto a mindset of poverty and believing "I only need God to meet my basic needs" be considered a self-focused perspective rather than a truly godly one?

_____
_____
_____
_____
_____
_____

Why is God's desire to prosper you not about you but about your purpose? What does that look like, practically?

_____
_____
_____
_____
_____
_____

How does the story of Moses's call to build the tabernacle with resources he didn't yet have inspire you to trust that God will pull the resources you need to accomplish His purposes from somewhere outside of what's available to you?

_____
_____
_____
_____
_____

What dreams has God placed on your heart that require resources you don't currently have? Considering what you've read so far, where might you start in order to secure them?

_____
_____
_____
_____
_____
_____
_____
_____

What larger purpose do you envision your prosperity serving, and how can you collaborate with God to make that vision a reality?

_____
_____
_____
_____
_____
_____
_____

According to your current priorities, are you in a place where money would liberate and bless or destroy and curse?

_____
_____
_____
_____
_____
_____
_____

CHAPTER 6

PAY YOUR TITHE

> **WE FAIL TO OBEY GOD IN OUR FINANCES BECAUSE WE FAIL TO TRUST GOD WITH OUR FINANCES.**

REVIEW, REFLECT, AND RESPOND

As you read Chapter 6: "Pay Your Tithe" in *Creating Your Own Economy*, review, reflect on, and respond to the text by answering the following questions.

_____
_____
_____
_____
_____

Reflect on your current attitude toward tithing. Do you see it as an act of obedience, worship, or obligation? How has this mindset shaped your willingness to tithe?

_____
_____
_____
_____
_____

Think about a time when you were hesitant to tithe or gave inconsistently. What fears or doubts influenced your decision, and what was the result?

_____
_____
_____
_____
_____

When you consider God's promises about tithing, what emotions arise? Do they challenge your faith, inspire hope, or create discomfort? Why?

_____
_____
_____
_____
_____
_____
_____
_____

> *"Bring the whole tithe into the storehouse, that there may be food in my house. Test me in this," says the Lord Almighty, "and see if I will not throw open the floodgates of heaven and pour out so much blessing that there will not be room enough to store it."*
>
> **—Malachi 3:10 (NIV)**

Consider the scripture above and answer the following questions:

How do you interpret the phrase "bring the whole tithe"? Are there aspects of your tithing where you've been hesitant or giving just enough to feel like you've fulfilled an obligation?

_____
_____
_____
_____
_____
_____

Reflect on a time when you gave sacrificially. Did you notice any changes in your relationship with God or your circumstances? How did it influence your readiness to tithe then and moving forward?

_____
_____
_____
_____
_____
_____

How would you evaluate your obedience to God's Word regarding money, and how might that be connected to your current financial situation?

_____
_____
_____
_____
_____
_____

What specific excuses or justifications have you made for not tithing, and how do they reflect deeper struggles in your faith or priorities?

_____
_____
_____
_____
_____
_____

How has your understanding of tithing evolved over time? Are there any past beliefs or teachings about tithing that you need to unlearn or refine?

_____
_____
_____
_____
_____
_____

If God's blessings in your life are tied to your faithfulness in tithing, what changes do you feel called to make to align more closely with His principles?

_____
_____
_____
_____
_____
_____

From where or from whom do you seek financial guidance first? In what ways has relying on worldly advice shaped your financial decisions, and how has that impacted your trust in God as your provider?

_____
_____
_____
_____
_____
_____

Why is God's promise to bless us financially contingent upon whether we honor our commitments to follow His financial laws?

Do you have a generous spirit? How do you respond to the idea that a lack of generosity can hinder a person's ability to prosper?

Have you ever had a bad experience with giving, and how has that discouraged you from living generously? What role does wisdom play in giving above and beyond your tithe?

CHAPTER 7

DETERMINE TO DO THE WORK

> IF WE DO THE DIFFICULT PART, GOD WILL DO THE IMPOSSIBLE PART.

REVIEW, REFLECT, AND RESPOND

As you read Chapter 7: "Determine to Do the Work" in *Creating Your Own Economy,* review, reflect on, and respond to the text by answering the following questions.

What role does action play in receiving God's blessings? How much of your time is spent praying and confessing for financial blessings versus actively taking steps toward achieving them?

_____
_____
_____
_____
_____
_____
_____
_____

How do you reconcile the concept of working diligently while also trusting God to provide the results?

_____
_____
_____
_____
_____
_____
_____
_____

Every believer is at a different point in their faith journey regarding money, and taking action can look very different for each person. What does taking action look like for you and your family to step into the blessings God has planned for your life?

_____

_____

_____

_____

_____

_____

_____

_____

> **"And let us not grow weary of doing good, for in due season we will reap, if we do not give up."**
> **—Galatians 6:9 (ESV)**

Consider the scripture above and answer the following questions:

This verse highlights that a harvest comes from consistently "doing good." What do you think Paul means by "doing good," and how does it apply to your current efforts?

_____

_____

_____

_____

_____

_____

_____

How do you react when it feels like your efforts are going unrewarded? Does your trust in God's promise from this verse falter in those moments? What drives you to give up before seeing the results?

_____
_____
_____
_____
_____
_____

The chapter discusses embracing discipline and sacrifice. What specific sacrifices do you feel God is calling you to make in order to achieve the outcomes He has planned for you?

_____
_____
_____
_____
_____
_____

What blessings has God placed in your life right now that you can be thankful for? How regularly do you take time to express your gratitude to Him for those things?

_____
_____
_____
_____
_____
_____

The chapter discusses embracing discipline and sacrifice in your efforts to create wealth. What sacrifices have you made or are you willing to make to open yourself up to receive from God?

_____
_____
_____
_____
_____
_____
_____
_____

Like Peter, we are encouraged to take small, active steps towards living a prosperous life. When have you seen significant blessings result from small acts of faithfulness, either in your own life or in the life of someone you know?

_____
_____
_____
_____
_____
_____
_____
_____

Have you ever found yourself treating God like a genie, expecting Him to grant all your desires? How has this chapter and previous chapters reframed your understanding of who God is and what He expects from us in the area of finances?

_____
_____

How do you see yourself reflected in the invalid at the Pool of Bethesda (John 5) as you consider his interaction with Jesus?

How does the phrase, "If we do the difficult part, God will do the impossible part," encourage and challenge you to take action in areas where you've been hesitant?

CHAPTER 8

GIVE AND PROSPER

> YOU DON'T ALWAYS REAP WHERE YOU SOW, BUT YOU DO ALWAYS REAP WHAT YOU SOW.

REVIEW, REFLECT, AND RESPOND

As you read Chapter 8: "Give and Prosper" in *Creating Your Own Economy*, review, reflect on, and respond to the text by answering the following questions.

Where have you experienced the principle of sowing and reaping in your life—both positively and negatively?

_____
_____
_____
_____
_____
_____
_____

What are you sowing right now—in your work, your finances, marriages, and your relationships? What are you hoping to see happen as a result? What promises of God can you confess to reinforce the action as you wait for the harvest?

_____
_____
_____
_____
_____
_____
_____
_____

This chapter states, "You don't always reap where you sow, but you do always reap what you sow." What does this statement mean to you, and can you share a personal example of it in action?

_____
_____
_____
_____
_____
_____
_____
_____

> *"I have fought the good fight, I have finished the race, I have kept the faith. Now there is in store for me the crown of righteousness, which the Lord, the righteous Judge, will award to me on that day—and not only to me, but also to all who have longed for his appearing."*
>
> —2 Timothy 4:7-8 (NIV)

Consider the scripture above and answer the following questions:

What is the difference between doing "favors" for people and "blessing" people? Where in your life have you seen this distinction?

_____
_____
_____
_____
_____

How does knowing that your reward is sure influence you to bless others?

_____
_____
_____
_____
_____
_____

Meditate on the concept that "God never blesses nothing; He always blesses something." What does this mean to you?

_____
_____
_____
_____
_____
_____

What seeds are you storing or locking inside a vault? How does understanding that God multiplies the seeds you sow challenge your decision to keep them locked away?

_____
_____
_____
_____
_____
_____

Which of your own appetites are you trying to feed by consuming the seed God has given you instead of sowing it?

___

When you give, do you give reluctantly or with a cheerful heart? Do your actions show whether you truly believe that God cannot be out-given?

___

How does it impact you to know that God not only blesses what you sow but also protects what is yours from the enemy? How could embracing this truth transform your life?

_____
_____
_____
_____
_____
_____
_____
_____
_____
_____

How much does your church or circle of influence emphasize the principle of giving? Where do you see this principle modeled, and what are the implications of that for God's mandate to give?

_____
_____
_____
_____
_____
_____
_____
_____
_____
_____

CHAPTER 9

ESTABLISH YOUR TRUE MOTIVES

> GOD PUT US ON THIS EARTH, NOT TO SEE HOW MUCH WE COULD GATHER, BUT TO SEE HOW MUCH OF HIS LOVE WE MIGHT SPREAD TO OTHERS.

REVIEW, REFLECT, AND RESPOND

As you read Chapter 9: "Establish Your True Motives" in *Creating Your Own Economy,* review, reflect on, and respond to the text by answering the following questions.

_____
_____
_____
_____
_____

Reflect on your current motives for seeking financial success or blessings. Are they rooted in a desire to serve and love God's people or to fulfill personal ambitions? How does this realization challenge you?

_____
_____
_____
_____
_____

Think about a time when your motives for giving or pursuing success were questioned, either by others or within yourself. What did that experience reveal about the state of your heart?

_____
_____
_____
_____
_____

The chapter discusses how pure motives align with God's will. What specific desires or intentions in your life might need refining to truly align with His purposes?

_____
_____
_____
_____
_____
_____
_____
_____

> *"If I give everything I own to the poor and even go to the stake to be burned as a martyr, but I don't love, I've gotten nowhere."*
>
> —1 Corinthians 13:3 (MSG)

Consider the scripture above and answer the following questions:

Think about a time when you gave generously or made a significant sacrifice. How did love—or the lack of it—affect the impact of your actions on others and on your own spiritual growth?

_____
_____
_____
_____
_____
_____

What does this scripture reveal about the connection between the heart and actions? In what ways does this truth apply to your life?

_____
_____
_____
_____
_____
_____

Reflect on an act of generosity where your true motives became clear only in hindsight. What did you learn about yourself from that experience?

_____
_____
_____
_____
_____
_____

Think about a time when God revealed impure motives in your heart. How did you respond, and what changes did you make as a result? What might He be revealing about your motives now in the area of giving?

_____
_____
_____
_____
_____
_____

The chapter highlights that pure motives lead to lasting blessings. What does this say about the importance of consistent giving that flows out of a pure heart?

_____
_____
_____
_____
_____
_____
_____
_____
_____
_____

How do you know when you are giving out of love versus personal gratification?

_____
_____
_____
_____
_____
_____
_____
_____
_____
_____
_____
_____

What distinguishes biblical love from worldly love? Can you recall a time when you showed biblical love to someone who was difficult to love? How do action and emotion play different roles in the concept of cheerful giving?

_____
_____
_____
_____
_____
_____
_____
_____
_____
_____

Why does knowing the heart of God compel us to love others more deeply and give out of pure motives?

_____
_____
_____
_____
_____
_____
_____
_____
_____
_____

Do you view your work as meaningful, and how does the quality of your efforts reflect that belief, even if you don't enjoy your current job?

_____
_____
_____
_____
_____
_____
_____
_____
_____
_____
_____
_____
_____
_____
_____

In what ways does generosity act as God's "preventative medicine" for selfishness and covetousness? What stands out to you about that statement, and in what ways does it resonate with you?

_____
_____
_____
_____
_____
_____

What key principles from this book have been most impactful for you, and how do you plan to incorporate them into your life?

CREATING YOUR OWN ECONOMY

www.ingramcontent.com/pod-product-compliance
Lightning Source LLC
Chambersburg PA
CBHW062123080426
42734CB00012B/2960